the guide to owning a

Miniature Pinscher

Jackie O'Neil

T.F.H. Publications, Inc.
One TFH Plaza
Third and Union Avenues
Neptune City, NJ 07753

ISBN 0-7938-1891-5

www.tfh.com

Contents

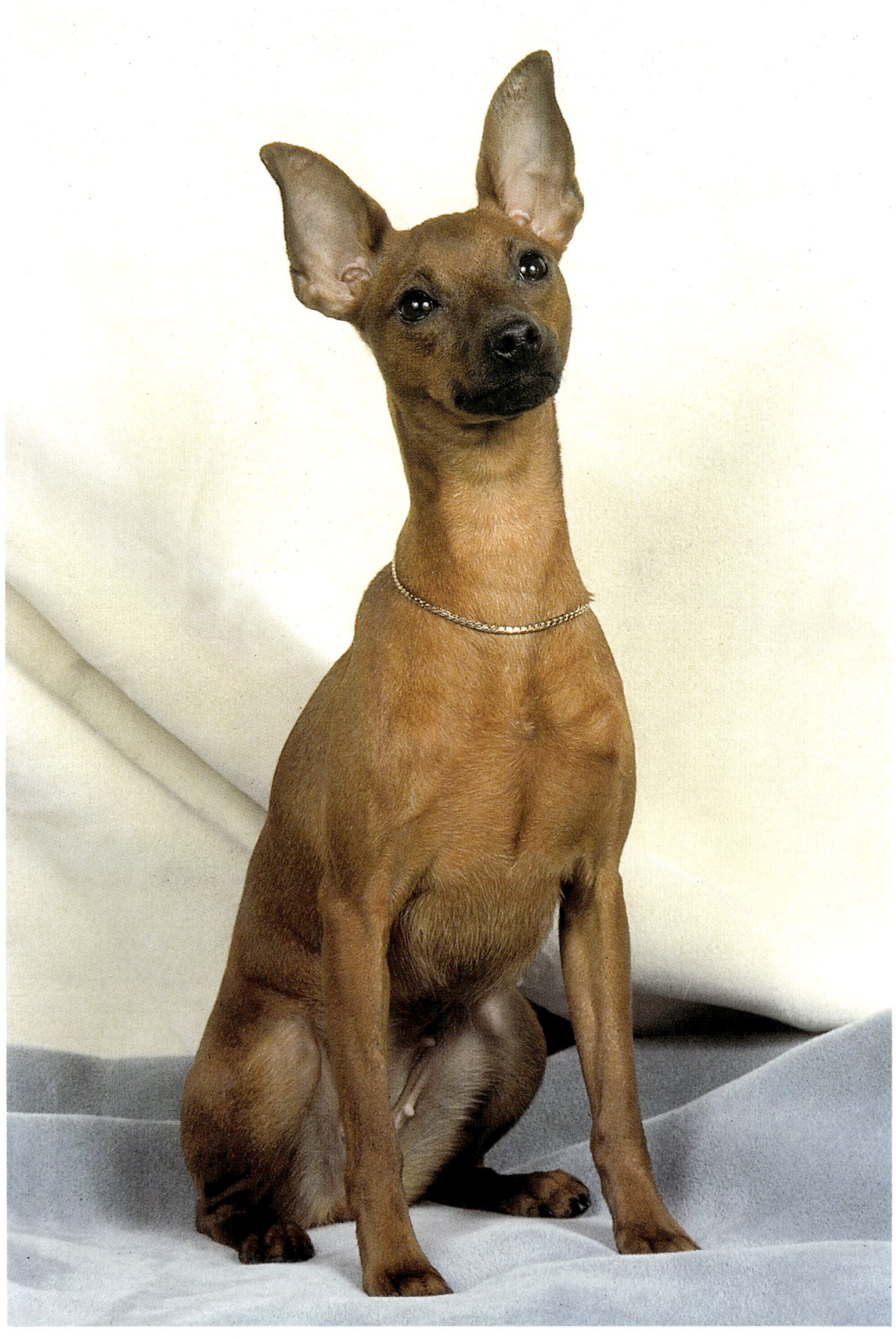

The Miniature Pinscher, known as the "Min Pin" by his admirers, is quite a big little dog. His vim and assertiveness has earned him the reputation of a spirited and dauntless companion.

The History of the Miniature Pinscher

Perhaps the best thumbnail description of the Miniature Pinscher, or Min Pin as he is affectionately known to his fanciers, is "A lot of dog in a little body." This lively little dog displays few of the characteristics expected of a toy dog.

Many persons who are unfamiliar with the background of the breed consider it a "scaled-down" version of the larger Doberman Pinscher, which it resembles in conformation and color. Although the ideal Miniature Pinscher should resemble the Doberman, it is not bred down from that variety. Both the Doberman Pinscher and the Miniature Pinscher were developed in Germany in the latter part of the 19th century, and both are believed to have a large portion of the English Black-and-Tan Terrier in their ancestry. However, the Doberman and the Min Pin are separate and distinct breeds.

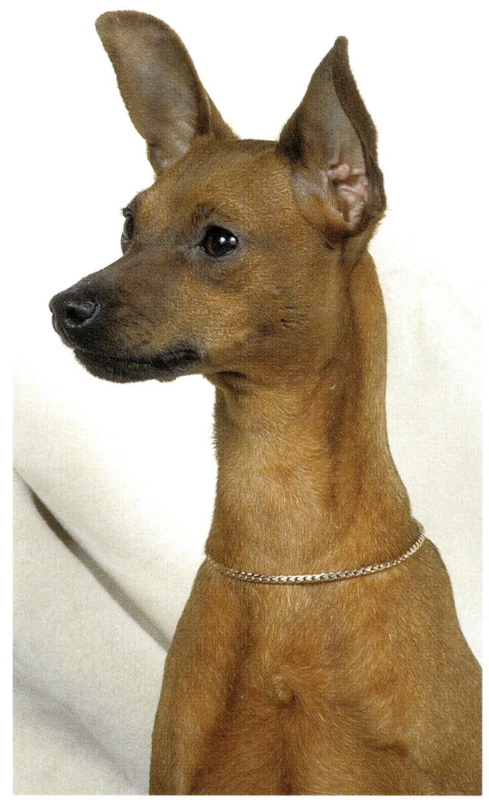

Although the Min Pin is considered a "scaled-down" version of the Doberman Pinscher, it is not bred down from that variety. The ideal Min Pin should, however, resemble the Doberman in many ways.

Small dogs that are very similar to the Miniature Pinscher have been known to exist in Germany and in the Scandinavian countries for several centuries. The breed was not really standardized until 1895 when the Pinscher Klub was formed in Germany and set up stud records and standards for the breed. The Min Pin has gained in popularity, and since the early 1900s, has even threatened the Dachshund's status as the favorite German dog.

For several years before World War I, the Miniature Pinscher was healthy, balanced, sound, and beautiful and still retained his popular appeal thanks to Berta and his followers. Breed historians consider the years around 1910 as the "Golden Years" for the breed. During that period, as many as 60 splendid and physically fit Miniature Pinschers were often found competing at a single show.

EFFECTS OF THE WAR YEARS

World War I did tremendous damage to the breed. Because food was difficult to obtain, the German people found an alert and brave small dog much easier to maintain than a larger watchdog. Demand for the breed was high, enticing profiteers to become breeders. With no concern for quality and caring only for money, the profi-

Min Pins are extremely individualistic—there is something unique and wonderful about each one, be she shy, outgoing, rowdy, or pensive.

Min Pins, when brought up together, revel in one another's company. In general, they are gregarious and friendly, despite their "protective" instincts.

teers kept up with the demand by breeding inferior dogs. The results were more inferior specimens, which were bred to other deficient dogs, and once again, the breed deteriorated. By the end of the war, many Miniature Pinschers were weak and timid, and the German Kennel Club wisely refused to register the breed until it regained its soundness and spirit. Unregistered dogs don't bring much money, so the profiteers lost interest in the breed, leaving the loyal supporters to repair the damage.

With the help of Judge Berta, the determined, devoted breeders prevailed again. "Power and Warmth" became the slogan for their breeding programs as they attempted to correct their breed's ills and recreate a healthy, sound, and confident small dog. By 1924, German experts were once again praising the breed.

The breed's seesaw struck the ground again when World War II also caused overpopularity. The profiteers returned and thousands of sad specimens were produced, resulting in another decline in quality. This time, besides small, weak specimens, there was a proliferation of larger, coarse dogs. However, recovery was rapid following the war. Once again, the Pinscher-Schnauzer Klub tightened its regulations. Before litters were permitted registration, an expert evaluated them, and even though the

Although most Miniature Pinschers are as alike as twins, there is a wide variety in acceptable coat colorings.

sire and dam were registered, the puppies had to be of good quality to rate their "papers." During 1945, only 76 Miniature Pinschers were accepted for registration, but the 705 Miniature Pinschers that were added to the record in 1947 signaled the breed's quick recovery.

THE MIN PIN IN THE UNITED STATES

Old family photographs that include Miniature Pinschers prove the breed arrived in the US at least as early as 1900. Like many breeds of foreign origin, the first dogs accompanied their immigrating families.

The American Kennel Club (AKC) accepted the Miniature Pinscher for registration on March 31, 1925. A "black, red, and brown" female named Asta von Sandreuth, registration number #454601, was the first dog of the breed to be AKC registered. She was whelped in Germany on June 5, 1924 and imported to the US by her American owner, Mrs. B. Seyschab.

The AKC recognized the Miniature Pinscher Club of America in 1929, and Min Pins were officially classified in the Terrier Group. However, the Miniature Pinscher Club of America was not happy with that designation and petitioned the AKC to reclassify the breed. A year later, Min Pins were placed in the Toy Group and called the Pinscher (Miniature). The official name of the breed was changed to Miniature Pinscher in 1972.

A VARIETY OF COLORS

Most Miniature Pinschers are as alike as twins; it is said that only a person who loves one dog can tell it from another. Nevertheless, there is a wide variety of acceptable coat colors.

In the original standard of the German Pinscher Klub, permissible colors included black with rust or yellowish markings as the preferred coat; chocolate or brown with yellowish or rust markings as the second choice; and red as acceptable, but least desired. Also approved was the harlequin, which is white with spots of black, chocolate, or red. Later, the harlequin was dropped from the standard. Although a harlequin may be registered with the American Kennel Club (AKC), it will not be admitted into the show ring.

In the US, the red coat became the most popular, and breeders devoted much time to developing strains with lustrous reddish coats. In the past years, however, the blacks with rust markings regained popularity and may be found at many kennels and at shows.

A MANUFACTURED BREED

Many of the most desirable traits of the Miniature Pinscher are because

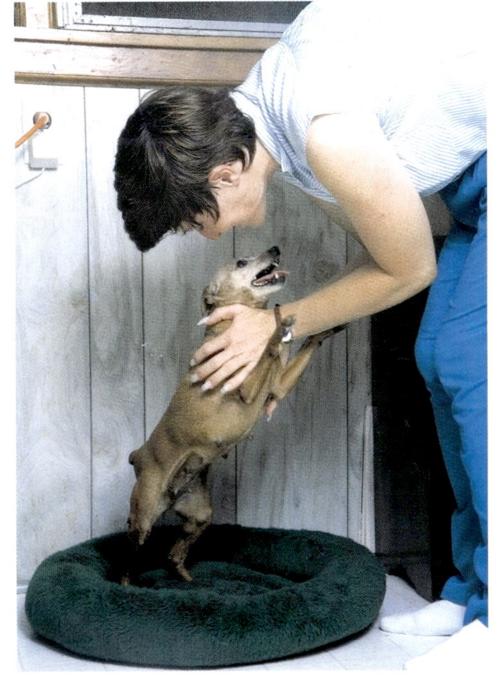

Considered a "manufactured breed," the Miniature Pinscher, one might then infer, has been "homemade" to meet the specifications outlined by the praise-worthy German breeders who created it.

this breed has been "manufactured" to meet specifications. His liveliness, alertness, and boldness, his neat, clean appearance, and his faithfulness and affection for his pet person are the results of many generations of careful breeding. Although there have been dogs similar to the Min Pin for centuries, his present type is a tribute to the thoroughness of the German breeders. About 1870, Louis Dobermann of Thuringia, Germany began the selective breeding that produced the Doberman Pinscher. He wanted a large dog, built on terrier lines and with the terrier's grace and agility, but a dog with the strength of a working shepherd or draft dog. At the same time, other German breeders were working to develop such breeds as the Boxer, the German Shepherd Dog, and the Giant Schnauzer.

As soon as the large Doberman Pinscher was established as a breed that would produce its own type, fanciers of smaller dogs began working toward a dog in the 5- to 10-pound class that would encompass the traits and the appearance of the Doberman. They were so successful that the Miniature Pinscher appeared as a dog that would run true to type even before the Doberman itself received official recognition as a distinct breed.

A POPULAR PET

Miniature Pinschers are rapidly gaining more fans every year. With so many Americans living in apartments and condominiums, a stylish small dog with the alert attitude and brave demeanor of a large one is very much in demand. In 1985, the AKC registered 3,143 Miniature Pinschers and ranked the breed at 47th in popularity. A decade of steady ascent made the Miniature Pinscher the 19th most popular breed in 1995—17,810 Min Pins were registered that year. In 2003, the Min Pin is still ranked as the 19th most popular breed with 15,230 dogs being registered in 2002.

While some profiteering types have jumped on the Min Pin bandwagon, the majority of modern Min Pins look and act like their nickname, the "King of Toys." The Miniature Pinscher Club of America is made up of dependable breeders representing the length and breadth of our country, and a multitude of local breed clubs are also dedicated to preserving, protecting, and improving the breed. When buying a Min Pin, look for a breeder who is active in one of these clubs. This is the best way to avoid the profiteers and acquire a happy and healthy Miniature Pinscher.

Characteristics of the Miniature Pinscher

Stylish and saucy, the Miniature Pinscher's proud carriage and regal gait earned it the nickname "King of Toys." Often referred to as "a big dog in a little package," these small dogs are surprisingly brave. The breed standard mentions the Miniature Pinscher's "fearless animation, complete self-possession, and spirited presence," and these characteristics are as much a part of the breed's persona as its unique physical appearance and proud gait. A correct Miniature Pinscher exudes self-confidence, not only in the privacy of his home or cradled in the safety of his owner's arms, but also when walking on lead down a busy street, when passing other dogs in the park, and when accompanying his owner to friends' homes.

Originally classified by the American Kennel Club (AKC) as a terrier, the Miniature Pinscher still retains terrier-type tenacity. Urban dogs seldom have the opportunity to stalk anything larger than a low-flying moth, but their rustic relatives still enjoy the chase and reportedly catch rabbits bigger than themselves as well as smaller rodents. Reveling in the hunt, they also have the persistence to wait out their prey, and

The Min Pin is the "King of Toys," standing proud and "tall" above all of the other toy breeds.

many of them exhibit the terrier tendency to determinedly dig their quarry out of the ground.

The Miniature Pinscher does not seem to recognize that he is small. In fact, your Min Pin won't hesitate to approach gigantic dogs in play and may even become aggressive with them. Always be cautious for your little dog. While a Min Pin is confident and brave, he is also vulnerable and sometimes has to be protected from his own brazen attitude toward larger animals. Most Min Pins believe they are a match for anything on four legs, and not all large dogs find this trait amusing.

The Miniature Pinscher is primarily a companion and housedog. Unable to tolerate cold temperatures or drafty basements, he needs cozy quarters near his human family and can get enough exercise even in a small apartment. When allowed outdoors, he should be in a securely fenced yard with sufficient shade, shelter, and fresh water. When taken for a walk, he should always be on lead. A well-conditioned Min Pin will be delighted to accompany his owner on long walks in pleasant weather but will prefer his cozy bed on rainy evenings and frosty winter mornings.

Min Pins love warmth and will contentedly curl up on a pillow by the fireplace, in a loving lap, or deep beneath the covers of your bed. In fact, these dogs seem to love the cozy feeling of something around them, and Min Pins are superior snugglers. Some owners who live in cold climates have successfully trained their dogs to use a kitty litter box during the worst winter months when the snowdrifts are higher than the tip of a Min Pin's ear. However, the dogs can be exercised outside during the winter if need be and will probably learn to "go" on lead very quickly in order to return to the comfort of indoor heating. Owners who exercise their Min Pins by turning them loose in fenced yards should be careful not to leave their dogs outside long enough to chill them. Bitter cold and bare bellies are not a good match.

The Miniature Pinscher is curious, alert, and joyful, with a high activity level and a well developed sense of fun. He retains his puppyish love of toys and games into old age, and it isn't unusual to see a vivacious, gray-muzzled "pup" play-killing his favorite squeaky toy and proudly strutting around the room with it. But the Min Pin doesn't have to be on the go all the time. This breed is also an accomplished lap-warmer and will be happy to watch television with you or help you read a book. While the Min Pin prefers an active lifestyle, he easily adapts to a more sedate household, especially if acquired young. In fact, Min Pins are beloved pets of thousands of senior citizens.

The highly adaptable Miniature Pinscher can be happy in a studio apartment or on a country estate. Small enough to create an exercise path of his own in even the tiniest

Your Min Pin needs to be kept busy in order to stay out of trouble. You can keep him from becoming bored and destructive by providing him with many different types of chew toys, such as those made by Nylabone®.

apartment, a Min Pin may suddenly take off on a mad-cap race and do several laps around the living room sofa. Min Pins also enjoy playing with children, provided the youngsters have been taught how to safely and gently handle a pet. Children should enjoy their Min Pin with adult supervision until they are old enough to realize that dogs have intelligence and feelings rather than battery-operated toys made for pulling and poking.

Alert watchdogs with an extremely keen sense of hearing, Miniature Pinschers recognize the sound of their owners' vehicles and footsteps but are quick to bark a warning when strange cars pull up to the house or unfamiliar footsteps draw near. It is not unusual or wrong for a Miniature Pinscher to be somewhat reserved toward visiting strangers and possessive about his human family. However, an ideal Min Pin will accept his owner's friends within a reasonable time and will start demanding some attention from them. When away from his home territory, this breed should be outgoing toward friendly strangers and inspect new places with courageous curiosity.

Just because the Min Pin is diminutive doesn't mean it won't become noisy or find his way into trouble when left to his own devices. The same qualities that make the Miniature Pinscher so charming—spirit, energy, and confidence—can turn a neglected or untrained Min Pin into a tiny terror. Don't get a dog at all if you don't have time to give him the vital gift of basic training. Dogs are social animals and need guidance and companionship. There are many other types of pets available that readily adapt to long hours of solitude.

The expression of the Miniature Pinscher is undoubtedly one of intelligence and audacity. Many believe that of all the breeds in the Toy Group, the Min Pin is surely the boldest and most intelligent.

Socialization brings out the best in a Miniature Pinscher's personality. It means familiarizing a puppy (or new dog) with the people, animals, objects, and noises he may encounter during everyday life. Vaccinated puppies should be introduced to friendly people of all ages and both sexes and to non-menacing, well-mannered dogs. They should ride in cars other than for trips to the veterinarian; walk on varied footing, such as linoleum, concrete, grass, wood, and carpet; and encounter bicycles, shopping carts, joggers, people in wheelchairs, and traffic sounds—all while on lead, of course. If a Miniature Pinscher lacks early socialization, he may never trust anyone who isn't part of his immediate human family.

Training a Miniature Pinscher is fun because the breed learns fast and has excellent retention. Most Min Pins are happy and willing workers, but because this breed is both inquisitive and clever, he can test the patience of his trainer. Seldom satisfied to do obedience work in the prescribed fashion, the Min Pin sometimes seems to try new things just to test his owner's reaction. Just when you think your dog learned a particular trick or obedience exercise, he may come up with a comical way around it. Owners who stay calm and use patient persistence and lots of praise eventually end up with marvelously trained Min Pins. These dogs are terrific hams and relish attention, so keep the kudos coming and your Min Pin will continue performing with obvious pleasure. Many Min Pins excel at competitive activities such as showing, obedience, and agility, or rewarding avocations such as therapy work.

Living with a Miniature Pinscher is never boring. Extremely fun loving, this breed greets each day with renewed cheer, and some owners swear their dogs spend the night dreaming up new ways to tease. A happy, healthy Min Pin moves with quick, deft agility and never goes anywhere at a walk that can be reached at a run. He enjoys his toys, and whether his owner chooses to join in the games or simply watch, the spectacle is entertaining. With the spirit of a large working dog and a bark that is bigger than he is, the Miniature Pinscher is a superb small dog for anyone who wants a little one with the heart of a hero.

The Standard for the Miniature Pinscher

The Miniature Pinscher, like all other purebred dogs, is measured against a breed standard of perfection—a written description of what the ideal specimen should look like. Each dog-registering organization draws up a standard for each breed of dog it recognizes; however, these standards vary in the way they are worded from registry to registry and from country to country.

THE AKC STANDARD FOR THE MINIATURE PINSCHER

General Appearance—The Miniature Pinscher is structurally a well balanced, sturdy, compact, short-coupled, smooth-coated dog. He naturally is well groomed, proud, vigorous and alert. Characteristic traits are his hackney-like action, fearless animation, complete self-possession, and his spirited presence.

Size, Proportion, Substance—*Size*—10 inches to 12 1/2 inches in height allowed, with desired height 11

Breed standards vary from country to country and from registry to registry. Become familiar with the standard that applies to your country and registry.

inches to 11 1/2 inches measured at highest point of the shoulder blades. *Disqualification*—Under 10 inches or over 12 1/2 inches in height. Length of males equals height at withers. Females may be slightly longer.

Head—In correct proportion to the body. Tapering, narrow with well fitted but not too prominent foreface which balances with the skull. No indication of coarseness. *Eyes* full, slightly oval, clear, bright and dark even to a true black, including eye rims, with the exception of chocolates, whose eye rims should be self-colored. *Ears* set high, standing erect from base to tip. May be cropped or uncropped. *Skull*

The eyes of the breed are full, slightly oval, almost round, clear, bright, and dark, even to a true black.

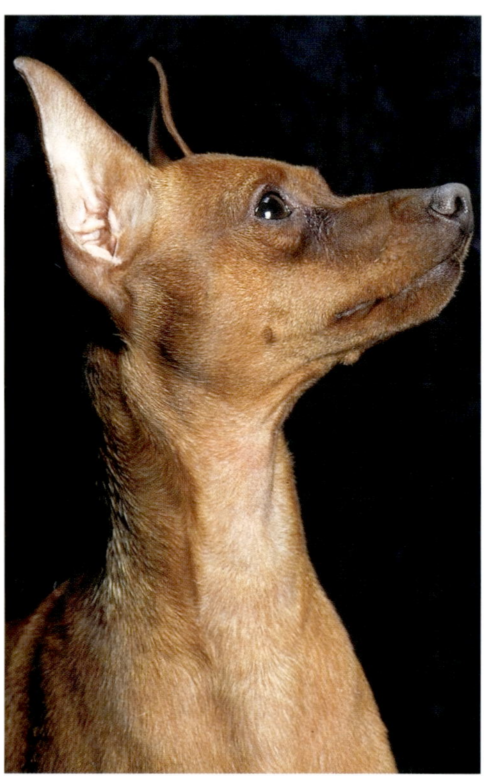

The standard calls for the neck to be proportioned to the head and body, slightly arched, and gracefully curved.

appears flat, tapering forward toward the muzzle. *Muzzle* strong rather than fine and delicate, and in proportion to the head as a whole. Head well balanced with only a slight drop to the muzzle, which is parallel to the top of the skull. *Nose* black only, with the exception of chocolates which should have a self-colored nose. *Lips and Cheeks* small, taut and closely adherent to each other. *Teeth* meet in a scissors bite.

Neck, Topline, Body—*Neck* proportioned to head and body, slightly arched, gracefully curved, blending into shoulders, muscular and free from suggestion of dewlap or throatiness.

Topline—Back level or slightly sloping toward the rear both when standing and gaiting. *Body* compact, slightly wedge-shaped, muscular. *Forechest* well developed. Well-sprung *ribs* . Depth of brisket, the base line of which is level with points of the elbows. Belly moderately tucked up to denote grace of structural form. Short and strong in *loin* . *Croup* level with topline. *Tail* set high, held erect, docked in proportion to size of dog.

Forequarters—*Shoulders* clean and sloping with moderate angulation coordinated to permit the hackney-like action. Elbows close to the body. *Legs*—Strong bone development and small clean joints. As viewed from the front, straight and upstanding. *Pasterns* strong, perpendicular. *Dewclaws* should be removed. Feet small, catlike, toes strong, well arched and closely knit with deep pads. *Nails* thick, blunt.

Hindquarters—Well muscled quarters set wide enough apart to fit into a properly balanced body. As viewed from the rear, the *legs* are straight and parallel. From the side, well angulated. *Thighs* well muscled. *Stifles* well defined. *Hocks* short, set well apart. *Dewclaws* should be removed. *Feet* small, catlike, toes strong, well arched and closely knit with deep pads. *Nails* thick, blunt.

Coat—Smooth, hard and short, straight and lustrous, closely adhering to and uniformly covering the body.

Color—Solid clear red. Stag red (red with intermingling of black hairs). Black with sharply defined rust-red markings on cheeks, lips, lower jaw, throat, twin spots above eyes and chest, lower half of forelegs, inside of hind legs and vent region, lower portion of hocks and feet. Black pencil stripes on toes. Chocolate with rust-red markings the same as specified for blacks, except brown pencil stripes on toes. In the solid red and stag red a rich vibrant medium to dark shade is preferred. *Disqualifications*—Any color other than listed. Thumb mark (patch of black hair surrounded by rust on the front of the foreleg between

Different coat colorings are acceptable for the Min Pin.

The Miniature Pinscher's conformation is sturdy and well balanced. The gait is high-stepping, reaching, moving freely and easily—true hackney-like action is desired. The dog should drive smoothly and strongly from the rear.

the foot and the wrist; on chocolates, the patch is chocolate hair). White on any part of dog which exceeds one-half inch in its longest dimension.

Gait—The forelegs and hind legs move parallel, with feet turning neither in nor out. The hackney-like action is a high-stepping, reaching, free and easy gait in which the front leg moves straight forward and in front of the body and the foot bends at the wrist. The dog drives smoothly and strongly from the rear. The head and tail are carried high.

Temperament—Fearless animation, complete self-possession, and spirited presence.

DISQUALIFICATIONS

Under 10 inches or over 12 1/2 inches in height.

Any color other than listed. Thumb mark (patch of black hair surrounded by rust on the front of the foreleg between the foot and the wrist; on chocolates, the patch is chocolate hair). White on any part of dog which exceeds one-half (1/2) inch in its longest dimension.

Approved July 8, 1980

Reformatted February 21, 1990

Selecting Your Miniature Pinscher

The purchase of any dog is an important step, and the well-cared-for Miniature Pinscher will live with you for many years. Once the prospective Miniature Pinscher owner decides that he is definitely ready for the responsibilities of dog ownership, he will undoubtedly want to rush out and purchase a puppy right away. This is not a good idea. It is extremely important that anyone considering taking home a Miniature Pinscher thoroughly researches the breed. You must be certain that a Miniature Pinscher will fit in with your family, home environment, and lifestyle.

It is very important that your Miniature Pinscher be purchased from a breeder who has earned a reputation for consistently producing dogs that are physically healthy and mentally sound. Breeders earn that reputation for quality by selectively breeding their dogs. Selective breeding aims to maintain the virtues of a breed and eliminate genetic weaknesses. The American Kennel Club can assist a prospective dog buyer in

Selecting the right Min Pin should not be a quick decision. Remember that this dog will be living with you for many years to come.

finding a responsible breeder of quality stock.

The responsible Miniature Pinscher breeder will breed for good temperament far ahead of any other characteristic and will ensure that his or her puppies are properly socialized. The socialization process should not be overlooked. Proper socialization will help produce a mentally stable dog that will be able to get along with all kinds of people and other animals. A well-socialized Miniature Pinscher will not show fear, shyness, or aggressiveness. Because Miniature Pinscher pups need human contact right from the beginning, it is important that the breeder spend a lot of time with each puppy individually to establish the human/canine relationship.

With any luck, you will be able to find a reputable breeder residing in your area who will not only be able to provide the right Miniature Pinscher for you, but who will also have the parents of the puppy on the premises. Meeting the parents of the puppy gives you an opportunity to see firsthand what kind of dogs your puppy comes from. The parents of the puppy should be certified with the Orthopedic Foundation for Animals (OFA) as free of hip dysplasia and the Canine Eye Registration Foundation (CERF) as free of hereditary eye diseases such as cataracts and progressive retinal atrophy. Good breeders are not only willing to have you see the dam (mother) and sire (father) of the litter, but also to inspect the facility in which the dogs are raised. These breeders will also be able to discuss with you any genetic problems that exist in the breed, how they deal with these problems, and how they take measures to safeguard against them.

Do not be surprised if a concerned breeder asks lots of questions about you, your family, and the environment in which your Miniature Pinscher will be raised. Good breeders are just as concerned that their dogs are going to good homes as you, the buyer, are

When visiting a breeder, her Min Pins should look healthy and loved. They should not shy away from people.

Before selecting the right Min Pin for your family, you will have to visit many different breeders.

in obtaining a well-adjusted, healthy dog. The breeder will use all the information you give him to match the right puppy with the right home. For example, a quiet, single adult generally needs a puppy with a different personality from the Miniature Pinscher that is appropriate for a household full of young and energetic children. A person who takes home a Miniature Pinscher should be able to provide him with the exercise and positive outlets that this breed requires. The time you spend in making the right selection ensures you get the right dog for your lifestyle.

If there are no local breeders in your area, there are legitimate and reliable breeders throughout the country that will appear on the national kennel club lists. These established breeders safely ship puppies to different states and even different countries. Always check the references of these breeders and do not hesitate to ask for documentation of their answers. The breeder will undoubtedly have as many questions for you as you will have for him or her. Getting all the information you can to the breeder will ensure that you get the pup with the temperament best suited for you.

Familiarize yourself with the breed standard before making your selection. This will help you in choosing a show-quality or pet-quality Min Pin.

Most breeders will not allow their puppies to go to their new homes until after they have been given their first vaccinations—usually at about nine weeks of age. Once weaned, your pup is highly susceptible to many infectious diseases that can be transmitted through people. It is best to make sure your puppy is fully inoculated before he leaves the breeder's residence. You should continue his immunization schedule with your veterinarian.

When arriving at the breeder's home or kennel, the buyer should look for cleanliness in both the dogs and the areas in which the dogs are kept. The cleanliness of the dogs and the condition of the area in which they sleep and play strongly indicate how well the breeder treats the puppies.

A healthy, little Miniature Pinscher puppy should be strong and sturdy to the touch, neither too thin nor obese and bloated. The coat should be shiny and clean, with no sign of dry or flaky skin. The puppy's eyes should be clear, bright, and free of redness or irritation. The inside of the puppy's ears should be pink—discharge or a bad odor could indicate ear mites or infection. A pup that coughs, has diarrhea, or has any eruptions on the skin is usually ill and should not be considered. In fact, if one puppy shows signs of illness, the health of the whole litter must be questioned.

As you are making a commitment to the puppy for his lifetime, make sure he reacts positively toward you and members of your family. Select the puppy that seems outgoing and ready to trust you. Sit down with the puppies and see which one is interested in playing. If you are looking for strictly a companion pet, pick the puppy that wants to be with you and enjoys your company. Take the puppy you are interested in away from his littermates into another room or another part of the kennel. The smells will remain the same for the puppy, so he should still feel secure and maintain his personality, but it will give you an opportunity to inspect the puppy more closely without distractions. If the puppy ignores you or seems more interested in going back to his littermates, choose another one.

When you purchase your Miniature Pinscher, remember that the purchase of any purebred dog entitles you to three very important documents: a copy of the dog's pedigree, a health record containing an inoculation schedule, and the dog's registration certificate.

Does your family have the time for a new Min Pin puppy? If not, consider adopting an adult dog.

HEALTH RECORD

The Miniature Pinscher breeder that you buy your puppy from should have initiated the necessary inoculation series for the litter by the time they are eight weeks of age. These inoculations protect the puppies against hepatitis, leptospirosis, distemper, and canine parvovirus. In most cases, rabies inoculations are not given until a puppy is four months of age or older.

These inoculations are given as a series and it is very important that your Miniature Pinscher puppy receives the full set in order for them to be effective. The veterinarian you choose will then be able to continue on an appropriate inoculation schedule.

PEDIGREE

The breeder must supply you with a copy of your Miniature Pinscher's pedigree, a document that authenticates your puppy's ancestors back to at least the third generation. All purebred dogs have a pedigree. The pedigree does not imply that a dog is of show quality, but is simply a chronological list of ancestors. The pedigree can be helpful in determining if your Miniature Pinscher's relatives have any titles in obedience or field trials, which can indicate their trainability and work ethic of the pup's parents and grandparents.

REGISTRATION CERTIFICATE

A country's governing kennel club issues this certificate. When you transfer the ownership of your

Upon making your final selection, the breeder should give you a copy of your Min Pin's pedigree, which should trace the dog's lineage back at least three generations.

These Min Pin pups may all look the same but each one has a distinct personality. Ask your breeder to examine each puppy away from his littermates to see the true temperament.

Miniature Pinscher from the breeder's name to your own name, the transaction is entered on this certificate. Once this is mailed to the kennel club, it is permanently recorded in their files. You will need to produce this document if you decide to show your Miniature Pinscher.

DIET

Most breeders will give the new owner a written record that details the amount and kind of food a puppy has been eating. Follow these recommendations exactly at least for the first month or two after the puppy comes to live with you. The instructions should indicate the number of times a day your puppy has been fed and the kind of vitamin supplementation he has been receiving, if any. If you follow the breeder's instructions it will greatly reduce the chance of your Miniature Pinscher puppy's suffering from an upset stomach and diarrhea.

The breeder's diet sheet should project the increases and changes in food that will be necessary as your puppy grows from week to week. If the breeder does not provide you with this information, ask your veterinarian for suggestions. If and when you decide to change the type or brand of dog food you are giving your Miniature Pinscher, do so gradually, mixing the old food with the new until the substitution is completed.

HEALTH GUARANTEE

Any reputable breeder will be more than willing to supply a written agreement that the puppy you choose to take home must be able to pass a veterinarian's examination. Further-more, the puppy should be guaranteed against the development of any hereditary problems. You should choose a veterinarian before deciding on your Miniature Pinscher and arrange an appointment with him right after you have picked up your puppy from the breeder and before you take the puppy home. If this is not possible, you should not delay this procedure any longer than 24 hours after the puppy leaves the breeder's residence.

SOCIALIZATION

A Miniature Pinscher's temperament is both hereditary and learned. A Miniature Pinscher pup can inherit a bad temperament from one or both of his parents and will definitely not make a good pet. Bad temperament can also be caused by a lack of socialization or mistreatment. The first step in getting a stable and well-adjusted companion is obtaining a happy puppy from a breeder who is determined to produce good temperaments and has taken all the necessary steps to provide early socialization. Your puppy should stay with his dam and littermates until at least eight weeks of age, because the interaction with them will help your Miniature Pinscher get along with other dogs later in life.

Once you bring your Miniature Pinscher puppy home, it is necessary to continue the socialization started by the breeder. You should introduce your Miniature Pinscher puppy to everyone, especially children. If you have young ones in your family, teach them to treat the puppy with respect. If you do not have children, find some gentle children to play with your puppy. Energetic children make wonderful playmates for the energetic Miniature Pinscher—and vice versa.

Take the puppy to as many different environments as you can—the beach, the park, the store, and the car. Expose him to different noises and situations, such as busy streets or crowded pet stores, always on lead, of course. Introduce him to other well-socialized dogs. All Miniature Pinschers must learn to get along with other dogs as well as with humans. Find a "puppy kindergarten" class in your area and attend regularly. Not only is it a great place to socialize you dog, but it is also the first step in training the new addition to your family.

Feeding Your Miniature Pinscher

Good nutrition is a necessary requirement in your Miniature Pinscher's life. Providing your dog with the proper diet is one of the most important aspects of caring for him. By carefully researching which diet is the best one, you can ensure his good health, which will affect all other parts of your life together.

The number of feedings and the amount fed will vary as your Min Pins get older. Ask your veterinarian or breeder for help in setting up a feeding schedule.

Your Min Pins should have manners when it is mealtime. Have your dogs assume the sit position until the food is placed down for them.

DOG FOODS

If you take a trip to your local pet emporium or supermarket, you cannot help but notice that there is an overwhelming selection of dog foods available. It can be confusing, to say the least, and it makes it hard to choose which brand is best for your Miniature Pinscher. There are certain things you should know about commercial dog food that will help you make the right decision. The more you educate yourself about what his nutritional needs are, the easier the decision will be.

In order to stay healthy, there are six essential nutrients that all dogs in every stage of life need in varied amounts: protein, fat, carbohydrates, vitamins, minerals, and water.

Protein

Protein can be burned as calories and stored as fat and helps with muscle growth, tissue repair, blood clotting, and immunity functions. Good sources of protein are meat, fish, poultry, milk, cheese, yogurt, fishmeal, and eggs.

Fat

Fat supplies the energy needed for the absorption of certain vitamins, provides insulation from cold, and makes food tastier. Fat can be found in meat and meat by-products and vegetable oils, such as safflower, olive, corn, or soybean.

Carbohydrates

Carbohydrates provide energy and keep intestines functioning smoothly. Complex carbohydrates are fiber and sugar and can be found in corn, oats, wheat, rice, and barley.

Vitamins

Vitamins are divided into two groups—water soluble and fat soluble. Different vitamins have different functions: vitamin A protects skin and promotes bone growth; vitamin B aids in metabolism; vitamin D aids in bone growth and increases calcium absorption; and vitamin K helps with blood clotting. Good sources of vitamins are fruit, vegetables, cereals, and the liver of most animals.

Minerals

Minerals provide strength to bone and ensure proper bone formation, maintain fluid balance and normal muscle and nerve function, transport oxygen to the blood, and produce hormones. Examples of minerals are calcium, phosphorus, copper, iron, magnesium, selenium, potassium, zinc, and sodium.

Water

The most important of all nutrients, water makes up over 60 percent of a dog. Water intake can come directly through drinking or can be released when food is oxidized. If your dog's diet is lacking in water, dehydration can occur, which can lead to serious breakdown of organs or even death. All dogs must retain a water balance, which means that their total intake of water should be in balance with the total output. Make sure that your dog has access to cool, clean water at all times.

TYPES OF DOG FOOD

First, you should pick a dog food that is specially formulated for your dog. This will ensure that your Miniature Pinscher is getting the proper nutrition for growth and digestion. There are three types of dog food available on the market today, and all of them have good and bad points. You must choose the type that best fits your and your Miniature Pinscher's needs.

There are many different types of pet food in the stores today. Try to continue using a similar type to what was given by the breeder.

Dry Food

The good thing about dry food is that it is the least expensive, can conveniently be left in bowl for longer periods of time, and helps control tartar. However, it is the least appealing to dogs.

Canned food

Canned food is the most appealing to dogs, but it spoils quickly, is the most expensive, and requires more to be fed because the energy content is relatively low, especially for large or active breeds.

Semi-Moist

Semi-moist food will not spoil at room temperature and comes in prepackaged servings, but it also contains large amounts of sugar and preservatives in order to remain fresh without refrigeration.

Meals should be served at the same time every day. Your Min Pin will get used to the schedule that you set.

READING LABELS

There are two agencies that work together in regulating pet food labels. The first agency, the Association of American Feed Control Officials (AAFCO), is a non-governmental agency made up of state and federal officials from around the United States. They establish pet food regulations that cover areas like guaranteed analysis, nutritional adequacy statements, and feeding directions. Each state decides whether or not to enforce AAFCO's regulations. Most do; however, some do not.

The second agency, the Food and Drug Administration Center for Veterinary Medicine, establishes and enforces standards for all animal feed. This federal agency oversees aspects of labeling that covers proper identification of products, net quantity statements, and the list of ingredients.

Learn how to read dog food labels, especially when you consider how many brands are out there. Slight changes in wording can make the difference between a quality dog food and one that may not appear to be what it seems.

INGREDIENT LIST

Each ingredient contained in the dog

Fresh, clear water is as important to your Min Pin's health as is a nutritious dog food. Make sure he has plenty of water, especially on hot day.

food will be listed in descending order according to weight. However, the quality of each ingredient is not required to be listed. For best results, look for animal-based proteins to be high up on the list, such as beef, beef by-products, chicken, chicken by-products, lamb, lamb meal, fish meal, and egg. However, use caution and read carefully, because some manufacturers will manipulate the weight of products in order to place it higher or lower on the list. For example, they may divide the grains into different categories, like wheat flour and whole ground wheat, in order to lower the weight and make it seem less prominent on the ingredient list.

FEEDING INSTRUCTIONS

The feeding instructions on the dog food label are only suggestions; some dogs will eat more, some will eat less. Also, they are the amounts needed for the entire day, so you can divide it up the best way for you and your Miniature Pinscher. If you are not sure how much to feed, start off with the suggested amount and increase or decrease as necessary.

Although dog food labels tell you a lot about a product, there is a lot that they don't tell you. For example, some wording used on labels can be misleading. Foods that use the words "gourmet" or "premium" are not required to contain any higher quality

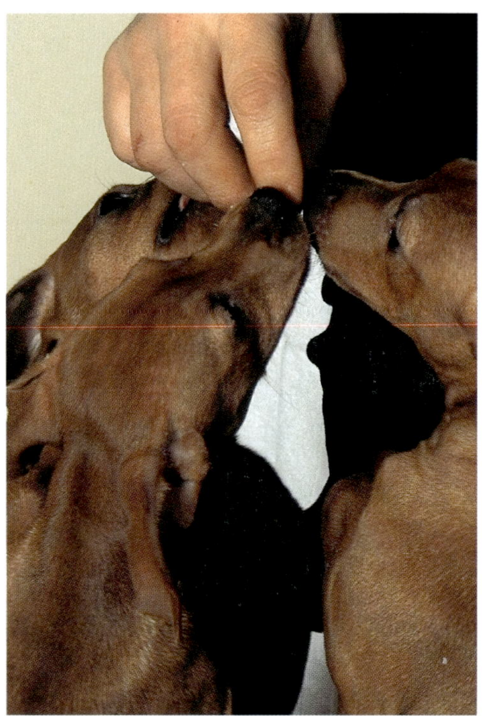

A good way to keep your Min Pins from overeating is to feed treats between meals. Just remember that these treats count toward total food consumption during the day so don't overdo it.

ingredients than any other product. Products that claim to be "all-natural" are not required to be. Some might think that this means the food is minimally processed or contains no artificial ingredients, but this is not necessarily true. In fact, all dog foods must contain some chemically synthesized ingredients in order to be deemed complete and balanced.

FEEDING YOUR MINIATURE PINSCHER PUPPY

If you are lucky, the breeder from whom you obtained your puppy will have given you a diet sheet, which will help you immensely with your feeding chores. A diet sheet will typically tell you the type of food your puppy has been eating, when he eats, and how to increase his food intake as he ages. Some breeders will even include enough food to get you through a day or two. If possible, follow this original feeding schedule as closely as possible and use the same brand of puppy food for the first few months. This will help avoid any stomach upsets or diarrhea. If you would like to change the brand of food your puppy is eating, do so gradually, slowly mixing the old food with the new food over a period of time until the old food is totally replaced.

If no diet sheet was provided for you, you will have to use the information available about dog food and choose one that is specially formulated for puppies. It should indicate that it is a growth formula as well. If you are undecided about which brand to choose, consult your veterinarian.

How will you know if you have made the right choice? First, take a look at your puppy's stool. It should be small and firm, not too loose or too dry. A large amount of stool means the food is not being digested. Although it may take a few months to notice, a puppy eating a nutritious diet will have all the signs of good health, including a glossy coat, high energy, and bright eyes.

WHEN TO FEED YOUR MINIATURE PINSCHER

For puppies, start off with light, frequent meals because your puppy's stomach is so small. If the breeder has included a feeding schedule with your diet sheet, follow that as closely as possible and make increases or decreases as recommended. If no feeding schedule accompanied your puppy, set one up right away.

A four-month-old (or younger) puppy should be fed four times a day. At four to six months of age, you can reduce the feedings to three, and after six months, you can start feeding once or twice a day, depending on your schedule. You should always feed him at the same time of day starting out with breakfast, lunch, mid-afternoon snack, and dinner, which should be served an hour before bedtime. Take your puppy, or even an adult Miniature Pinscher, outside to go potty as soon as he is finished with his meal.

Some people recommend "free feeding" your dog, which means leaving food out for him to nibble on all day. This makes it harder to judge exactly how much the dog has eaten and makes it harder to predict when the dog needs to go outside to eliminate. It also could lead to overeating, because many Miniature Pinscher will eat out of boredom. It is best to put the food down for your dog for a limited time and then take the food away when the time is up. Your Miniature Pinscher will adjust quickly to the schedule, and you'll have more control over the amount consumed.

HOW MUCH TO FEED

If you don't know the dog's prior feeding schedule, you will have to figure out how much to feed him. Start off by following the directions on the dog food label and increasing or decreasing the amount as needed. Give the recommended amount for your Miniature Pinscher's age and take it away after a period of time. If

Avoid feeding your Min Pins before or after exercising. Digestive problems may result.

Overfeeding will cause overweight Miniature Pinschers. A proper, nutritious diet will prevent them from getting fat.

your dog eats the food quickly and leaves nothing, you need to increase the amount. If there is leftover food, you may have to decrease the amount or feed smaller meals more frequently.

TREATS

Treats are a great way to encourage and reward your Miniature Pinscher for doing something well. There are plenty of treats available today that are not only tasty but also nutritious. Hard biscuits and Nylabones® can help keep his teeth clean. Remember to consider treats as part of your dog's total food intake. Limit the amount of treats you give your Miniature Pinscher, and be sure to feed him only healthy snacks. Avoid giving him table scraps, as they usually just add to his caloric intake. Obesity is a very serious health problem in dogs, so be sure to start your Miniature Pinscher off eating right.

BONES

Bones can help your dog with his overwhelming need to chew. They keep his teeth clean and keep him from becoming bored. Make sure you give your dog safe bones and toys made especially for dogs that will not splinter or break into tiny pieces. Pieces can be swallowed and become stuck in your Miniature Pinscher's intestinal tract or cause him to choke. Nylabone® makes safe, chewable, and edible dog bones, so give your Miniature Pinscher something fun and safe as a special treat.

SUPPLEMENTS

Healthy dogs that are fed a balanced diet will not need supplementation. In fact, some veterinarians believe that supplementing your Miniature Pinscher's diet with extra vitamins and minerals can aggravate conditions like hip dysplasia and hereditary skin problems. The only time you should give your puppy any kind of supplements is under the direction of your veterinarian and even then you should never exceed the prescribed amount.

Grooming Your Miniature Pinscher

A wash-and-wear breed, Miniature Pinschers need only a little grooming to absolutely glow. Condition your Miniature Pinscher from puppyhood to accept grooming as a regular part of life, and he will soon enjoy your touch and look forward to the attention. Talk to him softly while you work,

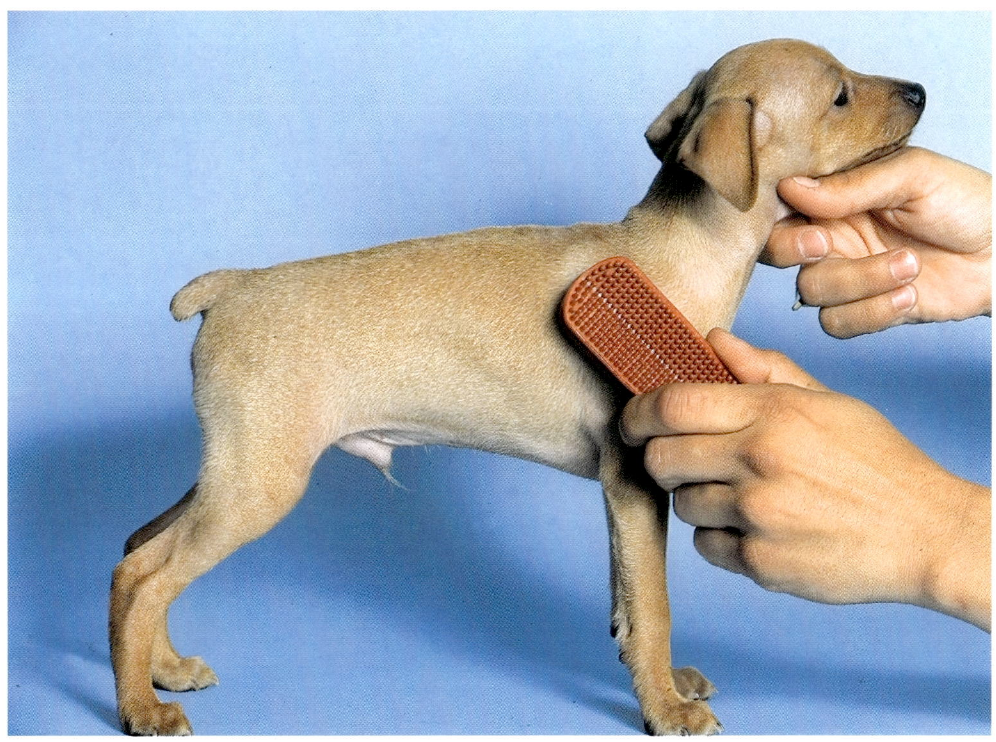

The Min Pin's short coat does not require much in the way of grooming. Regular brushing will help keep his coat looking its best.

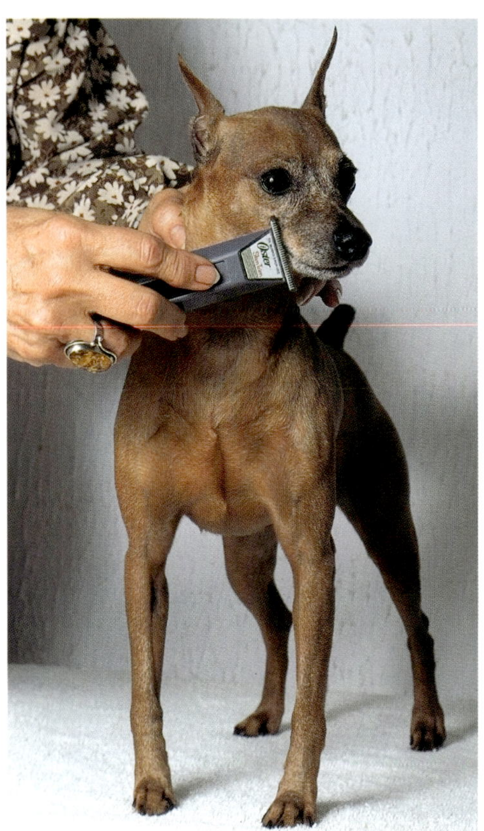

Grooming the Min Pin is no difficult chore. Some Min Pin owners opt to seek the service of a professional groomer while others take on the task themselves.

but if he becomes fidgety about being handled on any part of his body, say "No," sharply and firmly and continue grooming.

While you can groom your Miniature Pinscher on your lap, a grooming table may be easier on your back. In addition, standing on a table makes many dogs more cooperative. Grooming tables must be sturdy, have a non-slip surface such as ribbed rubber matting, and stand square without a hint of wobble. You can make one yourself or buy one at a dog show booth or through a pet-supply catalog. They are available in a variety of sizes, and the smallest is just right for a Miniature Pinscher. Most of the tables offered for sale have folding legs and are easy to move from one location to another. Some of them come with an adjustable arm and a loop that fits around the dog's neck to help keep him steady. Never leave your Min Pin alone on the table or even turn your back on him (especially if the loop is around his neck). It takes less than an instant for a dog to jump or fall, and the results are often tragic.

CARING FOR THE COAT

Start each grooming session with a brisk rubdown with your fingertips over the dog's whole body. This will loosen any dead skin. Then give him a thorough but gentle brushing. (A natural bristle brush is preferable to the nylon type.) First brush his coat against the grain, then with the grain. When you brush him, especially during the summer and fall months, check his coat for any signs of fleas, lice, or ticks. If you do find parasites, use a spray or dip to get rid of them.

When there are fleas, you will also have to change the dog's bedding and spray the areas of the house where he stays, paying close attention to cracks in the floor and along the baseboards. Repeat the de-fleaing treatment in about a week. Make sure the dog doesn't lick too much insecticide off his coat; if necessary, you can put a clown collar around his neck temporarily so he won't be able to reach his body with his tongue. Don't leave flea powder on too long, as it may be strong enough to burn his skin or coat.

If you find a tick, be sure to remove the entire insect. You can touch it with a drop of iodine to break its grip. Then lift it off with a pair of tweezers or a tissue and burn it or drop it into kerosene or gasoline to kill them.

If you find lice, small sucking and biting insects that attach themselves to the dog's body, you must apply a good pesticide regularly, burn all the dog's bedding, and thoroughly disinfect his living quarters.

BATHING YOUR MINIATURE PINSCHER

A normal, healthy dog should be bathed as *infrequently* as possible because a dog's skin is different from that of humans. It is very rich in oil glands and deficient in sweat glands. The oil keeps his skin soft and prevents it from drying and cracking. It also protects the coat and keeps it water-resistant. When a dog is bathed too often, the natural oil is removed from his skin, and the skin and coat can become dry. Minute cracks in the skin cause irritation, and the dog will scratch and bite himself, resulting in eczema or other infectious skin ailments.

Therefore, bathe your dog only when he gets so dirty that it is impossible to clean him any other way. When a bath is necessary, protect the dog's eyes and ears from water before putting him into the tub. Put a drop of petroleum jelly into each eye and plug his ears with cotton. The water should be lukewarm, never hot or cold. Use a shampoo specifically formulated for dogs and rinse all traces of soap from his coat. Then dry him with a thick towel, massage his coat with your hand, and brush him. If the day is warm and sunny, let him run outdoors to complete the drying, but if it is cold, keep him indoors.

NAIL CARE

Many dogs that run on gravel or pavement keep their toenails worn down, so they seldom need clipping. But a dog that doesn't do much running or runs on grass will grow long toenails that can be harmful. The long nails will force the dog's toes into the air and spread his feet wide. In addition, the nails may force the dog into an unnatural stance that can produce lameness.

You can control your dog's toenails by cutting them with a special dog clipper or by filing them. Many dogs object to the clipping, and it takes some experience to learn how to do it without cutting into the blood vessels (the quick). Your vet will probably examine your dog's nails whenever you bring him in and may trim them for you. He can show you how to do it yourself in the future.

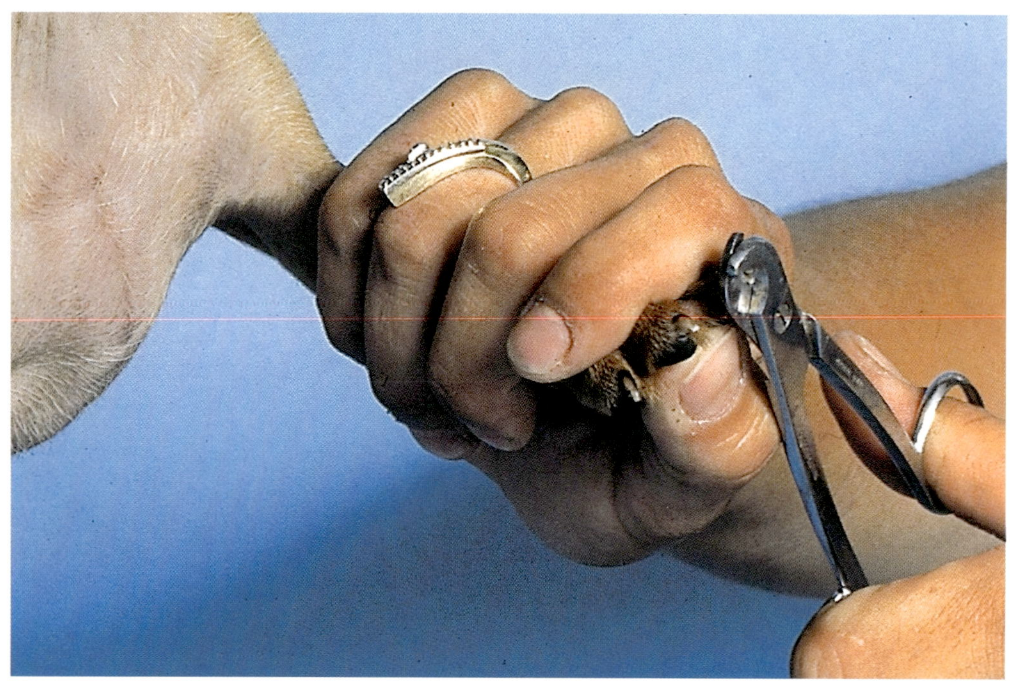

Nails should be attended to regularly. Clip with caution. Trim the end of the nail a little at a time to prevent injuring the quick.

If you prefer, you can file the points off your dog's nails every few weeks with a flat wooden file. Draw the file in only one direction—from the top of the nail downward in a round stroke to the end of the nail or underneath. You'll need considerable pressure for the first few strokes to break through the hard surface, but then it gets easier. You may also use an electric nail grinder, but make sure you accustom the dog to the noise it makes first.

Incidentally, it's a good idea to keep your Miniature Pinscher from walking on waxed or slippery floors, as this tends to break down the pasterns.

EAR CARE

Do not neglect your dog's ears when going through your grooming steps, because it is very important to his health. Ear infections can be caused by excessive dirt, moisture, and bacteria accumulating in the ear canal. When taking care of your Min Pin's ears, the first thing you should do is pluck or trim (with blunt-nosed scissors) the excess hair out. To keep them clean, use a cotton ball or washcloth dampened with commercial ear cleaner or mineral oil and wipe the inside of the earflap. If your dog's ear is sore, has excess wax, or has a bad smell, he probably has an ear infection and needs to see the veterinarian immediately.

Never stick anything into your Min Pin's ear canal. When cleaning, wipe the outside area of the earflap only, or you may damage your dog's eardrum.

EYE CARE

It is fairly easy to keep your dog's eyes clear, sparkling, and bright. First, make sure that you keep all debris (including hair) out of his eyes. Wipe you dog's eyes on a regular basis with a cotton ball or washcloth dipped in warm water. If your Min Pin's eyes appear red, cloudy, or swollen or have excess tearing, contact your veterinarian.

DENTAL CARE

All dogs and puppies need to chew. Chewing is an essential part of their physical and mental development, so you need to take good care of their teeth from the very beginning.

If you do not brush your dog's teeth on a regular basis, plaque builds up on the teeth and under the gums. If this plaque is not removed, periodontal disease, which is a bacterial infection, can occur. If left untreated, the bacteria can enter the bloodstream and spread to your dog's vital organs. Other problems can develop as well, such as mouth abscesses and tooth loss. Also, dogs that don't receive good dental care can suffer from really bad breath, a feature that does not endear them to humans or elicit affection.

It is much easier to brush your Min Pin's teeth than you may think, as long as you have the right supplies. You should purchase a dog toothbrush or a finger toothbrush (a rubber cap that fits over your index finger) and toothpaste made for dogs. Start by accustoming your dog to having your fingers in his mouth without brushing his teeth. When you are giving him his daily once-over, be sure to look in his mouth, lift his dewflaps to expose his gums, and touch his teeth. Soon this will become just another part of his grooming routine. Once he is used to this procedure, put some doggy-flavored toothpaste on the toothbrush and gently rub a few teeth at a time. Be sure to brush the tooth at the gum line.

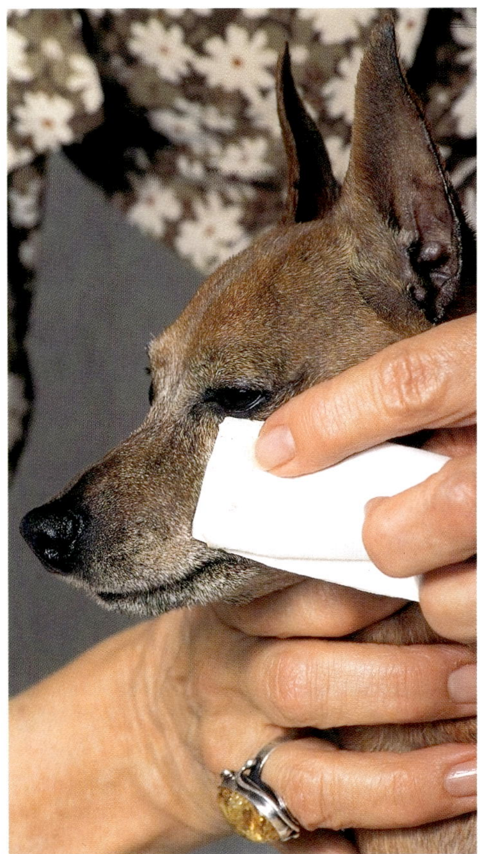

Keep your Min Pin's face clean. Use a soft cloth to wipe near the eyes.

Use a circular motion when brushing and slowly make your way around your dog's upper teeth. Make sure to get

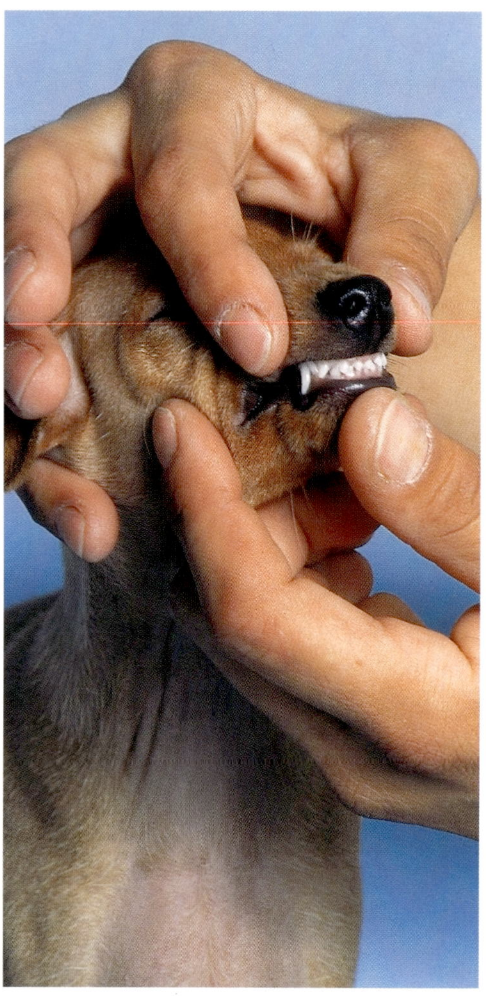

Checking your Min Pin's teeth should be a part of your grooming sessions.

the teeth in the back of the mouth, because these teeth are the ones most prone to periodontal disease. When you are finished with the top, do the bottom in the same manner.

Daily brushing would be ideal, but try to do it at least four times a week. This will ensure that your Min Pin keeps his teeth healthy and keeps them for a long time.

Chew Toys and Healthy Teeth

Your Miniature Pinscher, like all dogs, needs to chew. Chewing is a normal activity and helps to strengthen your dog's teeth. Many chew toys are designed to help clean your dog's teeth as he chews. The Nylabone® Dental Chew has raised tips that rub against the teeth and help to remove plaque. Another veterinarian-recommended product is Nylabone® Dental Chew Floss, which cleans between the teeth as your dog chews. No matter which chew toys you choose, make sure they are safe for your dog.

Training Your Miniature Pinscher

When you added a Miniature Pinscher to your family, you probably wanted a companion and a friend. You may have wanted a dog to go for walks, take jogs, or play with your children. Perhaps you wanted to get involved in dog shows or sports. To do any of these things, your

Every dog has the right to be trained. Teach your Min Pin exactly which behaviors are tolerated and which ones are not.

Miniature Pinscher will need training.

Good basic training will transform your jumpy, squirmy, wiggly little dog into a well-mannered Miniature Pinscher that is a joy to be around. A trained puppy or dog won't jump up on people, dash out the open door, or raid the trashcan. He will be able to be all you want him to be. Your dog needs to have someone tell him what to do. Your Miniature Pinscher has the right to be trained—it is unfair to leave him to figure out the human world on his own, and he won't be able to do it.

You, too, will benefit from training, because you will learn how to motivate your dog, how to prevent problem behavior, and how to correct mistakes that do happen. Dog training entails much more than learning the traditional sit, down, stay, and come commands—it means that you will be teaching your Miniature Pinscher to live in your house. You can set some rules and expect him to follow them.

HOUSEHOLD RULES

Start teaching your dog or puppy the household rules as soon as possible—preferably as soon as you get him home. Your eight- to ten-week-old puppy is not too young to learn what you expect of him. When you teach him these rules from the start, you can prevent bad habits from forming.

When deciding what rules you want him to follow, picture your puppy or dog the way you want him to be. It may be cute to let your little Miniature Pinscher sleep on your bed every night, but are you going to want a bedmate a year from now?

Take your Miniature Pinscher to the same area to eliminate each time.

Take a practical look at your dog and your environment and decide what behavior you can or cannot live with. It is important to make these decisions early in your dog's life, because what he learns as a puppy will remain with the adult dog.

HOUSETRAINING

If you have a puppy, one of the first things that you will undertake will be housetraining. You are teaching your dog that he has a specific place that he should eliminate, preferably outside. Your best bet is to start housetraining him as soon as possible. However, you need to remember that puppies between the ages of 8 to 16 weeks do not have control of their bladders or bowels. They are not able to "hold it" until they get a little older, which means that in the beginning, housetraining will take vigilance on your part. You will have to watch very carefully for signs that your puppy needs to eliminate. He will usually have to go to the bathroom after eating, drinking, sleeping, and playing. Most puppies will also give off signals, like circling or sniffing the floor. These behaviors are a sure sign that your puppy needs to go outside. When you see him display this behavior, don't hesitate. Carry your pup outside to the spot where you want him to eliminate. Praise your puppy for eliminating in the proper spot.

A crate, such as the Nylabone® Fold-Away Pet Carrier, makes crate training easier. Being confined to his crate for short periods of time will help him to learn better bowel and bladder control.

CRATE TRAINING

With the help of a regular schedule, you will be able to predict the times that your puppy will need to potty. The most useful thing that you can buy for your puppy to help facilitate this process is a crate. Training your puppy to use a crate is the quickest and easiest way to housetrain him, though it may be difficult to get an adult dog to use a crate if he's never used one before. Remember that your Miniature Pinscher will be developing habits throughout his training that will last him his lifetime—make sure you teach the right ones.

By about five weeks of age, most puppies are starting to move away from their mother and littermates to relieve themselves. This instinct to keep the bed clean is the basis of crate training. Crates work well because puppies do not want to soil where they eat and sleep. They also like to curl up in small dark places that offer them protection on three sides, because it makes them feel more secure. When you provide your puppy with a crate, you are giving him his very own "den"—to your puppy's inner wolf, it is home sweet home. Pups will do their best to eliminate away from their den, and later, away from your house.

Being confined in the crate will help a puppy develop better bowel and bladder control. When confined for gradually extended periods of time, the dog will learn to avoid soiling his bed. It is your responsibility to give your dog plenty of time outside the crate and the house, or the training process will not be successful.

Sometimes puppies really just need to get away from it all. The hustle and bustle of a busy household can be overwhelming at times. There are times when your puppy will get overstimulated and need to take a "time out" to calm down (especially if you have rambunctious kids around). A crate is great for all of these times. The crate can be used as your puppy's place of refuge. If he's tired, hurt, or sick, he can go back to his crate to sleep or hide. If he's overstimulated or excited, he can be put in his crate to calm down. If you are doing work around the house that doesn't allow you to watch over him, you can put him into his crate until you are done painting the bathroom or the workmen have left. In short, crates are lifesavers for puppy owners. Eventually, the puppy will think that it is pretty cool, too.

CHOOSING A CRATE

There are many types of crates to choose from. Consider what you will be using the crate for and pick the best one. The Nylabone® Fold Away Pet Carrier is a great choice because it folds up for easy storage when not in use and is perfect for traveling.

Buy a crate that will fit your dog's adult size. An adult dog should be able to stand up, turn around, and stretch out in the crate comfortably. However, you don't want your little puppy to have too much room to roam around in, either. This might become a problem, because he may decide to eliminate in one corner of his big, roomy crate and sleep in the other. The best thing to do is to block off a portion of the crate and make it progressively larger as your dog matures and grows.

INTRODUCING THE CRATE

Introduce your puppy to the crate

very gradually. You want the puppy to feel like this is a pleasant place to be. Begin by opening the door and throwing one of your puppy's favorite treats inside. You may want to teach him a command, like "bedtime" or "crate" when the pup goes into the crate. Let your dog investigate the crate and come and go freely. Don't forget lots of praise. Next, offer a meal in the crate. Put the food dish inside and after awhile, close the door behind him. Open the door when he's done eating. Keep this up until your puppy eats all his meals in the crate.

Soon your puppy will become accustomed to going in and out of the crate for treats and meals. If you do not wish to continue feeding him in his crate, you can start feeding elsewhere, but continue offering a treat for going into the crate. Start closing the door and leaving your puppy inside for a few minutes at a time. Gradually increase the amount of time your puppy spends in the crate. Always make sure that you offer him a treat and praise for going in. It is also a good idea to keep a few favorite toys inside the crate as well.

Crate Don'ts

Don't let your puppy out of the crate when he cries or scratches at the door. If you do, your dog will think that complaining will bring release every time. The best thing to do for a temper tantrum is to ignore the pup. Only open the door when the dog is quiet and has calmed down.

Don't use the crate as punishment. If you use the crate when he does something bad, your dog will think of the crate as a bad place. Even if you want to get the pup out of the way, make sure that you offer him lots of praise for going into the crate and give a treat or toy, too.

CRATE LOCATION

During the day, keep your puppy's crate in a location that allows him easy access and permits him to be part of the family. The laundry room or backyard will make a dog feel isolated and unhappy, especially if he can hear people walking around. Place it anywhere the family usually congregates—the kitchen or family room is often the best place.

At night, especially when your puppy is still getting used to the crate, the ideal place for it is in your bedroom, near your bed. Having you nearby will create a feeling of security and be easier for you as well. If the pup needs to go outside during the night, you can let him out before he has an accident. Your dog will also be comforted by the smell, sight, and sound of you, and will be less likely to feel frightened.

OUTSIDE SCHEDULE

As mentioned before, puppies need

Almost immediately after eating and drinking, your Min Pin pup will need to be taken outside to eliminate.

time to develop bowel and bladder control. The best way to most accurately predict when your Miniature Pinscher needs to eliminate is to establish a routine that works well for both of you. If you make a daily schedule of eating, drinking, and outside time, you will notice your Miniature Pinscher's progress.

Every person and family will have a different routine—there is no one right schedule for everyone. Just make sure that you arrange times and duties that everyone can stick with. The schedule you set will have to work with your normal routine and lifestyle. Your first priority in the morning will be to get the dog outdoors. Just how early this will take place will depend much more on your dog than on you. Once your Miniature Pinscher comes to expect a morning walk, there will be no doubt in your mind when he needs to go out. You will also learn very quickly how to tell your Miniature Pinscher's "emergency" signals. Do not test the dog's ability for self-control. A vocal demand to be let out is confirmation that the housetraining lesson is learned.

It is also important to limit your dog's freedom inside the house and keep a careful eye on him at all times. Many dogs, and especially puppies, won't take the time to go outside to relieve themselves because they are afraid that they will miss something; after all, everything exciting happens in the house. That's where all the family members usually are. When he is a puppy, you may, unfortunately, find your Miniature Pinscher sneaking off somewhere—behind the sofa or to another room—to relieve himself. By limiting the dog's freedom, you can prevent some of these mistakes. Close bedroom doors and put baby gates across hallways. If you can't supervise him, put the dog in the crate or outside in a secure area.

ACCIDENTS WILL HAPPEN

When housetraining your Miniature Pinscher, remember that if he has an accident in the house, it is not his fault; it's yours. It means that he was not supervised well enough or wasn't taken outside in time.

If you catch your dog in the act, don't yell or scold him. Simply say "No!" loudly, which should startle and stop him. Pick your pup up and go outside to continue in the regular relief area. Praise your puppy for finishing outside. If you scold or punish him, you are teaching him that you think going potty is wrong. Your dog will become sneaky about it, and you will find puddles and piles in strange places. Don't concentrate on correction; emphasize the praise for going potty in the right place.

If you find a little surprise left for you, do not yell at your puppy for it and never rub his nose in it. Your puppy will have no idea what you are talking about, and you'll only make him scared of you. Simply clean it up and be sure to keep a closer eye on him next time.

Housetraining is one of the most important gifts that you can give your dog. It allows him to live as one of the family. Every puppy will make mistakes, especially in the beginning. Do not worry—with the proper training and lots of patience, every dog can be housetrained.

BASIC TRAINING

Collar and Leash Training

Training a dog to a collar and leash is very easy and something you can start doing at home without assistance. Place a soft nylon collar on the dog. The dog will initially try to bite at it, but will soon forget it's there, more so if you play with him. Some people leave their dog's collar on all of the time; others put it on only when they are taking the dog out. If it is to be left on, purchase a narrow or round one so it does not mark the fur or become snagged on furniture.

Once the dog ignores his collar, you can attach the leash to it and let him pull it behind him for a few minutes every day. However, if your Miniature Pinscher starts to chew at the leash, simply keep it slack and let the dog

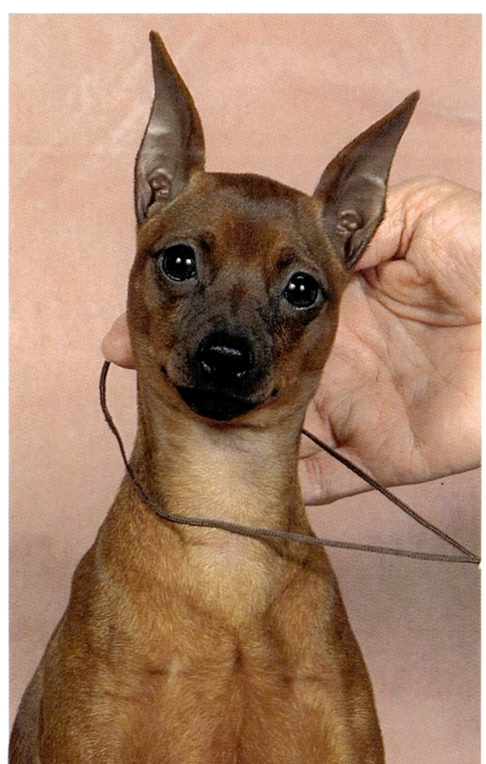

Training sessions should be done with your Min Pin wearing a collar and leash.

choose where to go. The idea is to let your dog get the feel of the leash, but not get in the habit of chewing it. Repeat this a couple of times a day for two days, and the dog will get used to the leash without feeling restrained.

Next, you can let the Miniature Pinscher understand that the leash will restrict his movements. The first time this happens, your dog will either pull, buck, or just sit down. Immediately call the dog to you and give him lots of praise. Never tug on the leash or drag the dog along the floor. This might cause the dog to associate his leash with negative consequences. After a few lessons, the puppy will be familiar with the restrictive feeling, and you can start going in a direction opposite from your Miniature Pinscher. Give the leash a short tug so that the dog is brought to a halt, call the dog to you enthusiastically, and continue walking. When your Miniature Pinscher is walking happily on the leash, end the lesson with lots of praise. There is no rush for your dog to learn leash training, so take as long as you need to make the dog feel comfortable.

Praise your Min Pin for successfully completing a command. The positive reinforcement will make him want to continue to please you.

BASIC COMMANDS

Begin training your Miniature Pinscher as soon as he is comfortable in your home and knows his name. There are two very important things to remember when training your Miniature Pinscher. First, train the dog without any potential distractions. Second, keep all lessons very short. Eliminating any distraction is important because it is essential that you have your puppy's full attention. This is not possible if there are other people, other dogs, butterflies, or birds to play with. Also, if you are training a puppy, always remember that puppies have very short attention spans. Even when the pup has become a young adult, the maximum time you should train him would be about 20 minutes. However, you can give the puppy more than

Your Min Pin must be taught that commands must be followed. Never give a command that you if you are not willing to enforce.

one lesson a day, three being as many as are recommended, each well apart. If you train any longer, the puppy will most likely become bored, and you will have to end the session on a down note, which you should never do.

Before beginning a lesson, always play a little game so that your Miniature Pinscher is in an active state of mind and more receptive to training. Likewise, always end lessons with playtime for the dog, and always end training on a high note, praising your dog. This will really build his confidence.

The Come Command

The come command is possibly the most important command you can teach your dog, and it is important to teach him this command as a puppy—it may even save your dog's life someday. Knowing that your dog will come to you immediately when you call him will ensure that you can trust him to return to you if there is any kind of danger nearby. Teaching your dog to come when called should always be a pleasant experience. You should never call your Miniature Pinscher in order to scold or yell at him, or he will soon learn not to respond. When the dog comes to you, make sure to give him a lot of praise, petting, and, in the beginning, a treat. If he expects happy things when he reaches your side, you'll never have trouble getting your dog to come to you.

Start with your dog on a long lead about 20 feet in length. Have plenty of treats that your Miniature Pinscher likes. Walk the distance of the lead, and then crouch down and say, "Come." Make sure that you use a happy, excited tone of voice when you call the dog's name. Your Miniature Pinscher should come to you enthusiastically. If not, use the long lead to pull him toward you, continuing to use the happy tone of voice. Give him lots of praise and a treat when he gets there. Continue to

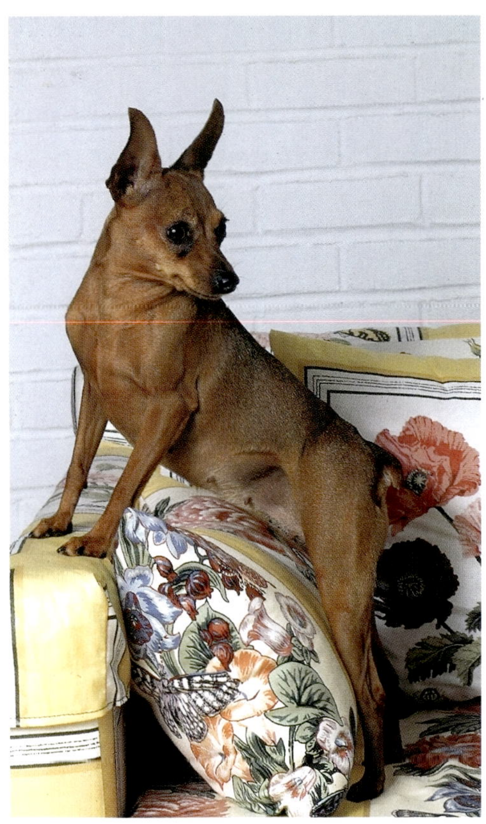

Training commands can begin almost as soon as you bring your new Min Pin home. Do not allow your dog to get away with behavior as a pup and expect him to obey as an adult.

use the long lead until your dog is consistently obeying your command.

The Sit Command

As with most basic commands, your Miniature Pinscher will learn the sit command in just a few lessons. One 15-minute lesson each day should do the trick in no time. Some trainers will advise you that you should not proceed to other commands until the previous one has been learned really well. However, a bright, young Miniature Pinscher is quite capable of handling more than one command per lesson and certainly per day. As time progresses, you will be going through each command as a matter of routine before a new one is attempted. This is so the dog always starts, as well as ends, a lesson on a high note, having successfully completed something.

When teaching the sit command, first, get a treat that your dog really likes and hold it right by his nose, so that all his attention is focused on it. Raise the treat above his head and say, "Sit." Usually, the dog will follow the treat and automatically sit. Give him the treat for being such a good dog and don't forget to praise him. After a while, your Miniature Pinscher will begin to associate the word "Sit" with the action. Most dogs will catch on very quickly. Once your dog is sitting reliably with the treat, take it away and just use praise as a reward. Most dogs will tend to stand up at first, so immediately repeat the exercise. When your Miniature Pinscher understands the command and does it right away, you can slowly move backward so that you are a few feet away. If he attempts to come to you, simply place the dog back in the original position and start again. Do not attempt to keep the dog in the sit position for too long. Even a few seconds is a long time for a impatient, energetic puppy, and you do not want him to get bored with lessons before he has even begun them.

The Stay Command

The stay command should follow your sit lesson, but it can be very hard for puppies to understand. Remember that a puppy wants nothing more than to be at your side, so it will be hard for him to stay in one place while you walk away. You should only expect your dog to perform this command for a few seconds at first, and then gradually work up to longer periods of time.

Face your dog and say, "Sit." Now step backward, saying, "Stay." It is also very helpful to use the hand signal for stay—place your hand straight out, palm toward the dog's nose. Let the dog remain in the position for only a few seconds before saying, "Come" and giving lots of praise and a treat. Once your dog gets the hang of it, repeat the command again, but step farther back. If your dog gets up and comes to you, simply go back to the original position and start again. As your dog starts to understand the command, you can move farther and farther back.

Once your Miniature Pinscher is staying reliably from a short distance, the next test is to walk away after placing the dog. This will mean your back is to the dog, which will tempt him to follow you. Keep an eye over your shoulder, and the minute the dog starts to move, spin around, say,

One of the easiest commands to teach your Min Pin is to sit. Help your pup into the proper position while giving the command.

"Stay," and start over from the original position.

As the weeks go by, you can increase the length of time the dog is left in the stay position—but two to three minutes is quite long enough for a puppy. If your puppy drops into a down position and is clearly more comfortable, there is nothing wrong with it. In the beginning, staying put is good enough!

The Down Command

From a dog's viewpoint, the down command is one of the more difficult ones to accept. This position is submissive in a wild pack situation. A timid dog will roll over, which is a natural gesture of submission. A bolder dog will want to get up and might back off, not wanting to submit to this command. The dog will feel that he about to be punished, which would be the position in a natural environment. Once he comes to understand this is not the case and that there are rewards for obeying, your Miniature Pinscher will accept this position without any problem.

You may notice that some dogs will sit very quickly, but will respond to the down command more slowly. This is their way of saying that they will obey the command, but under protest!

There are two ways to teach this command. If your dog is more willing to please, the first method should work. Obviously, with a puppy, it will be easier to teach the down if you are kneeling next to him. First, have your dog sit and hold a treat in front of his nose. When his full attention is on the treat, start to lower the treat slowly to the ground, saying "Down." The dog should follow the treat with his head. Bring it out slowly in front of him. If you are really lucky, your Miniature Pinscher will slide his legs forward and lie down by himself. Give him the treat and lots of praise for being such a good dog.

For a dog that won't lie down on his own (and most puppies won't), you can try this method: After the puppy is sitting and focused on the treat, take the front legs and gently sweep them forward, at the same time saying, "Down." Release the legs and quickly apply light pressure on the shoulders with your left hand. Then quickly tell the dog how good he is, give the treat, and make a lot of fuss. Repeat two or three times only in one training session. The dog will learn over a few lessons. Remember that this is a very submissive act on the dog's behalf, so there is no need to rush matters.

The Heel Command

All dogs should be able to walk nicely on a leash without a tug-of-war with their owners. Teaching your Miniature Pinscher the heel command should follow leash training. Heeling is best done in a place where you have a wall or a fence to one side of you, because it will restrict the dog's movements so that you only have to contend with forward and backward situations. Again, it is better to do the lesson in private and not in a place where there will be many distractions.

There will be no need to use a slip collar on your dog, as you can be just as effective with a flat, buckle one. The leash should be approximately 6 feet long. You can adjust the space between you, your Miniature Pinscher, and the wall so that your pet has only a small amount of room to move sideways. It is also very helpful to have a treat in your hand so that your dog will be focused on you and stay by your side.

Hold the leash in your right hand and pass it through your left. As the dog moves ahead and pulls on the leash, stop walking, and say, "Heel." Lure the dog back to your side with the treat. When the dog is in this position, praise him and begin walking again. Repeat the whole exercise. Once the dog begins to get the message, you can use your left hand (with the treat inside of it) to pat the side of your knee so that your Miniature Pinscher is encouraged to keep close to your side.

When your dog understands the basics, you can mix up the lesson a little to keep him focused. Do an about-turn, or make a quick left or right. This will result in a sudden jerk as you move in the opposite direction. The dog will now be behind you, so you can pat your knee and say, "Heel." As soon as the pup is in the correct position, give him lots of praise. The puppy will now begin to associate certain words with certain actions.

Once the lesson is learned and the dog is heeling reliably, then you can change your pace from a slow walk to a quick one, and your Miniature Pinscher will adjust. The slow walk is always the more difficult for most puppies, as they are usually anxious to be on the move. End the lesson when the dog is walking nicely beside you. Begin the lesson with a few sit commands so you're starting with success and praise.

Recall to Heel Command

When your dog is coming to the heel position from an off-leash situation—for instance, if he has been running free—he should do this in the correct manner. He should pass behind you and take up his position, then sit. To teach this command, have your Miniature Pinscher in front of you in the sit position with his collar and leash on. Hold the leash in your right hand. Give him the command to heel and pat your left knee. As the dog starts to move forward, use your right hand to guide him behind you. If you need to, you can hold the collar and walk the dog around the back of you to the desired position. You will need to repeat this a few times until the dog understands what is wanted.

The down command is a difficult one for your dog to learn. The down position in the dog's pack is a sign of being submissive.

When you have done this a number of times, you can try it without the collar and leash. If the dog comes up toward your left side, then bring him to the sit position in front of you. Hold his collar and walk the pup around the back of you. Your dog will eventually understand and automatically pass around your back each time. If the dog is already behind you when you recall him, then he should automatically come to your left side. If necessary, pat your left leg.

The No Command

The no command must be obeyed every time. Your Miniature Pinscher must understand it 100 percent. Most delinquent dogs—the jumpers, the barkers, and the biters—have never been taught this command. If your dog were to approach any potential danger, the no command, coupled with the come command, could save his life. You do not need a specific lesson for this command; it will most likely be used every day. You must be consistent and apply it every time your dog is doing something wrong. It is best, however, to be able to replace the negative command with something positive. This way, your dog will respond more quickly. For example, if your puppy is chewing on your shoe, tell him, "No!" and replace the shoe with a Nylabone®. Then give him lots of praise.

Your Healthy Miniature Pinscher

Dogs, like all other animals, are capable of contracting problems and diseases that, if listed, would seem overwhelming. However, in most cases these are easily avoided—meaning well-bred and well-cared-for animals are less prone to developing diseases and problems than are carelessly bred and neglected animals. Your knowledge of how to avoid problems is far more valuable than all of the books and advice on how to cure them. Respectively, the only person you should listen to about treatment is your vet. Veterinarians don't have all the answers, but at least they are trained to analyze and treat illnesses, and are aware of the full implications of treatments, which most others are not. This does not mean a few old remedies aren't good standbys when all else fails. In most cases, modern science provides the best treatments for disease.

Every Miniature Pinscher puppy should be vaccinated against the major canine diseases. These are distemper,

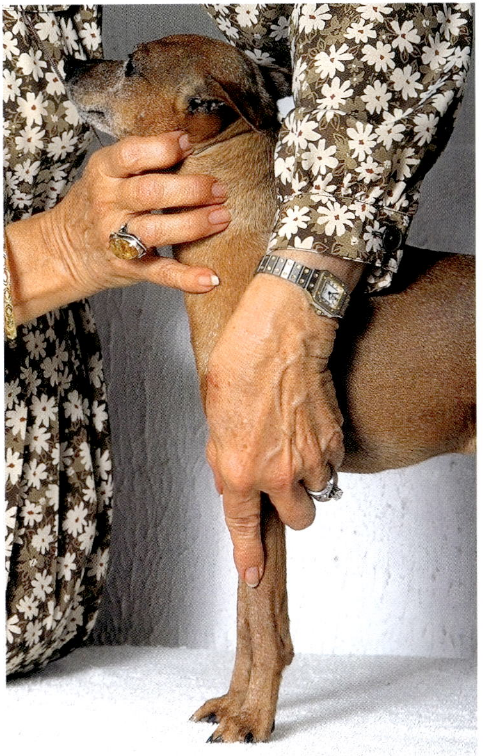

Regular visits to your veterinarian will keep your Min Pin in top health.

leptospirosis, hepatitis, and canine parvovirus. Your puppy may have received a temporary vaccination against distemper before you purchased him. Ask the breeder to be sure.

The age at which vaccinations are given can vary, but will usually be when the pup is 8 to 12 weeks old. By this time, any protection given to the pup by antibodies received from his mother's initial milk feeds will be losing its strength.

The puppy's immune system works on the basis that the white blood cells engulf and render harmless attacking bacteria. However, they must first recognize a potential enemy.

Vaccines are either dead or alive bacteria in very small doses. Either type prompts the pup's defense system to attack them. When a large attack comes (if it does), the immune system recognizes it and massive numbers of lymphocytes (white blood corpuscles) are mobilized to counter the attack. However, the ability of the cells to recognize these dangerous viruses can diminish over a period of time. It is therefore useful to provide annual reminders about the nature of the enemy. This is done by means of booster injections that keep the immune system on alert. Immunization is not a 100 percent guaranteed success in preventing illness, but it is very close. Certainly it is better than giving the puppy no protection.

Dogs are subject to other viral attacks. If there are high-risk factors in your area, your vet will suggest you have the dog or puppy vaccinated against these as well.

Your puppy or dog should also be vaccinated against the deadly rabies virus. In fact, in many places it is illegal for your dog not to be vaccinated. This is to protect your dog, your family, and the rest of the animal population from this deadly virus that infects the nervous system and causes dementia and death.

PHYSICAL EXAMS

Your Miniature Pinscher should receive regular physical examinations or checkups. These come in two forms. One is obviously performed by your vet, and the other is a day-to-day procedure that should be done by you. Apart from the fact that the exam will highlight any problem at an early stage, it is an excellent way of getting the dog used to being handled.

Check your dog's eyes, ears, nose, and mouth daily for any irritation or problems and be sure to keep them clean with regular grooming. Keep your dog's teeth healthy and his breath fresh by providing him with plenty of safe chew toys, like Nylabones®.

To do the physical exam yourself, start at the head and work your way around the body. You are looking for any sign of lesions or any indication of parasites on your Miniature Pinscher.

Always have a supply of safe chew toys for your dogs. Chew toys, such as those made by Nylabone®, will prevent destructive behavior as well as clean your Min Pin's teeth.

The most common parasites are fleas and ticks.

FIGHTING FLEAS

Fleas are very mobile and may be red, black, or brown in color. The adults suck the blood of the host, while the larvae feed on the adults' feces, which is rich in blood. Flea "dirt" may be seen on the pup as very tiny clusters of blackish specks that look like freshly ground pepper. The eggs of fleas may be laid on the dog, though they are more commonly laid off the host in a more favorable place, such as the bedding. They normally hatch in 4 to 21 days, depending on the temperature, but they can survive for up to 18 months if temperature conditions are not favorable. The larvae are maggot-like and molt a couple of times before forming a pupae, which can survive long periods until the temperature, or the vibration of a nearby host, causes them to emerge.

There are a number of effective treatments available. Discuss them with your veterinarian, and then follow all instructions for the one that you choose. Any treatment will involve a product for your dog and one for the environment. This will require diligence on your part to treat all areas and thoroughly clean your home and yard until the infestation is eradicated.

After walks in tall grass, inspect your Min Pin for ticks and other parasites. Parasite bites can irritate the skin and transmit disease.

THE TROUBLE WITH TICKS

Ticks are arthropods of the spider family, which means they have eight legs (though the larvae have six). They bury their headparts into the host and gorge on its blood. They are easily seen as small grain-like creatures sticking out from the skin. They are often picked up when dogs play in fields, but may also arrive in your yard via wild animals—even birds—or stray cats and dogs. Some ticks are species-specific; others are more adaptable and will host on many species.

The most troublesome type of tick is the deer tick, which spreads the deadly Lyme disease that can cripple a dog (or a person). Deer ticks are tiny and very hard to detect. Often, by the time they're big enough to notice, they've been feeding on the dog for a few days—-long enough to do their damage. Lyme disease was named for the area in which it was first detected—Lyme, Connecticut—but has now been diagnosed in almost all parts of the US. Your veterinarian can advise you of the danger to your dog(s) in your area, and may suggest your dog be vaccinated for Lyme. Always go over your dog with a fine-toothed flea comb when you come in from walking through any area that may harbor deer ticks. If your dog is acting unusually sluggish or sore, seek veterinary advice.

Attempts to pull a tick free will invariably leave the head part in the dog, where it will die and cause an infected wound or abscess. The best way to remove ticks is to dab a strong saline solution, iodine, or alcohol on them. This will numb them, causing them to loosen their hold, at which time they can be removed with tweezers. The wound can then be cleaned and covered with an antiseptic ointment. If ticks are common in your area, consult with your vet for a suitable pesticide to be used in kennels, on bedding, and on the dog.

SKIN DISORDERS

Apart from problems associated with lesions created by biting pests, a dog may fall foul to a number of other skin disorders, such as ringworm, mange, and eczema. Ringworm is not caused by a worm, but is a fungal infection. It manifests itself as a sore-looking bald circle. If your dog has any form of bald patches, let your veterinarian check him over; a microscopic examination can confirm the condition. Many old remedies for ringworm exist, such as iodine, carbolic acid, formalin, and other tinctures, but modern drugs are superior.

Fungal infections can be very difficult to treat, and even more difficult to eradicate, because of the spores. These can withstand most treatments, other than burning, which is the best thing to do with bedding once the condition has been confirmed.

Mange is a general term that can be applied to many skin conditions where the hair falls out and a flaky crust develops and falls away.

Often, dogs will scratch themselves, and this invariably is worse than the original condition, for it opens lesions that are then subject to viral, fungal, or parasitic attack. The cause of the problem can be various species of mites. These either live on skin debris and the hair follicles, which they destroy, or they bury themselves just beneath the skin and feed on the tissue. Applying general remedies from pet stores is not recommended because it is essential to identify the type of mange before a specific treatment is effective.

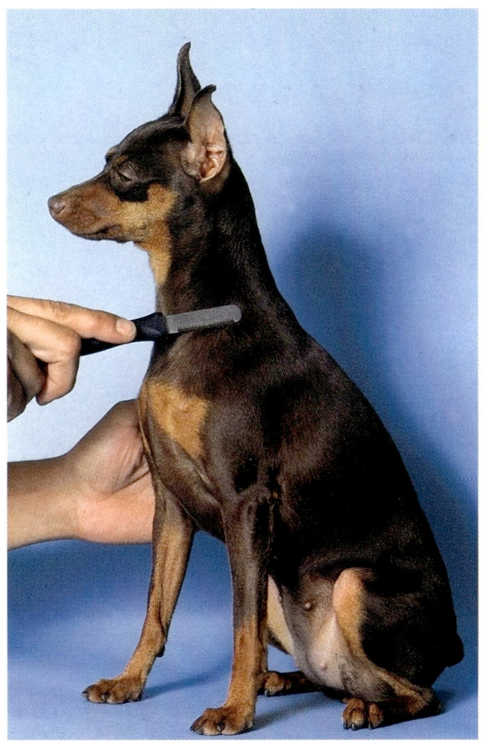

Check your Min Pin's skin whenever you brush her coat. If her skin is dry or irritated, call your vet.

Eczema is another non-specific term applied to many skin disorders. The condition can be brought about in many ways. Sunburn, chemicals, allergies to foods, drugs, and pollens—even stress—can all produce a deterioration of the skin and coat. Given the range of causal factors, treatment can be difficult because the problem is one of identification. It is a case of taking each possibility at a time and trying to correctly diagnose the matter. If the cause is dietary in nature, you must remove one item at a time in order to find out if the dog is allergic to a given food. It could, of course, be the lack of a nutrient that is the problem, so if the condition persists, you should consult your veterinarian.

WORMS

There are many species of worms, and a number of these live in the tissues of dogs and most other animals. Many create no problem at all, so you are not even aware they exist. Others can be tolerated in small levels, but become a major problem if they number more than a few. The most common types seen in dogs are roundworms and tapeworms. While roundworms are the greater problem, tapeworms require an intermediate host so they are more easily eradicated.

Roundworms of the species *Toxocara canis* infest the dog. They may grow to a length of 8 inches (20 cm) and look like strings of spaghetti. The worms feed on the digesting food in the dog's intestines. In chronic cases, the dog will become pot-bellied, have diarrhea, and vomit. Having passed through a stage when he always seems hungry, eventually, he will stop eating. The worms lay eggs in the dog that pass out in his feces. They are then either ingested by the dog, or are eaten by mice, rats, or beetles. The dog may then eat these and the life cycle is complete.

Larval worms can migrate to the womb of a pregnant bitch, or to her mammary glands, and this is how they pass to a puppy. The pregnant bitch can be wormed, which will help. The pups can, and should, be wormed when they are about two weeks old. Repeat worming every 10 to 14 days and the parasites should be removed. Worms can be extremely dangerous to young puppies, so you should be sure the pup is wormed as a matter of routine.

Tapeworms can be seen as tiny rice-like eggs sticking to the puppy or dog's anus. They are less destructive, but still undesirable. The eggs are eaten by mice, fleas, rabbits, and other animals that serve as intermediate hosts. They develop into a larval stage and must be eaten by the dog in order to complete the chain. Your vet will supply a suitable remedy if tapeworms are seen or suspected. The vet can also do an egg count on the dog's feces under the microscope; this will indicate the extent of an infestation.

There are other worms such as hookworms and whipworms that are also bloodsuckers. They will make a Miniature Pinscher anemic, and blood might be seen in the feces, which can be examined by the vet to confirm their presence. Cleanliness in all matters is the best preventative measure for all worms.

BLOAT (GASTRIC DILATATION)

This condition has proved fatal in many dogs, especially large and deep-chested breeds. However, any dog can get bloat. It is caused when gases build up in the stomach, especially in the small intestine. Carbohydrates are fermented and release gases. Normally, these gases are released by belching or by being passed from the anus. If for any reason these exits become blocked (such as if the stomach twists due to physical exertion), the gases cannot escape and the stomach simply swells and places pressure on other organs, sometimes cutting off the blood supply to the heart or causing suffocation. Death can easily follow if the condition goes undetected.

The best preventative measure is not to feed large meals or exercise your puppy or dog immediately after he has eaten. You can reduce the risk of flatulence by feeding more fiber in the diet, not feeding too many dry biscuits, and possibly by adding activated charcoal tablets to the diet.

Drinking too much water during meals may cause bloat. Mix dry food with some water to prevent excessive water consumption.

FIRST AID

All dogs will get their share of bumps and bruises, especially puppies, due to the rather energetic way they play. These will usually rectify themselves over a few days. Small cuts should be bathed with a suitable disinfectant and then smeared with an antiseptic ointment. If a cut looks more serious, stem the flow of blood with a towel or makeshift tourniquet, and rush your Miniature Pinscher to the veterinarian. Never apply too much pressure to the wound as it might restrict the flow of blood to the limb.

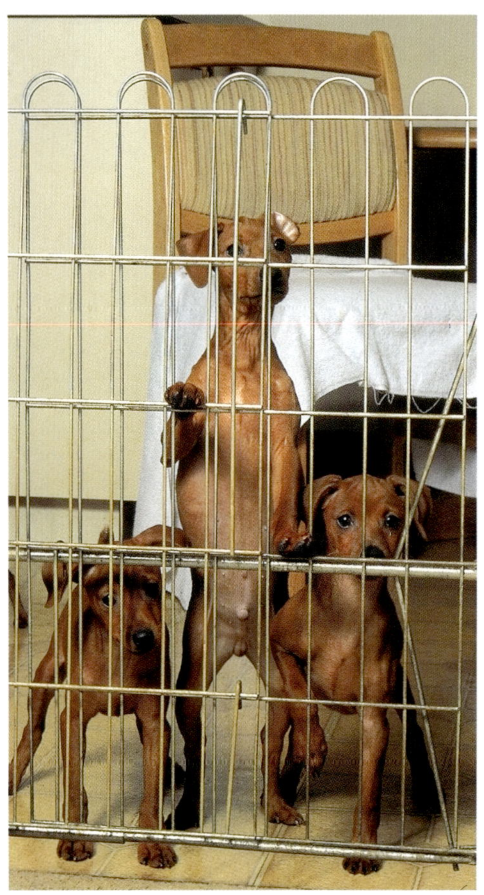

When you cannot supervise your Min Pin pups, make sure he is securely in his crate or in a fenced-in area. Accidents can happen when dogs are allowed to run freely.

In the case of burns, you should apply cold water or an ice pack to the surface. If the burn was due to a chemical, then this must be washed away with copious amounts of water. Apply petroleum jelly or any vegetable oil to the burn. Trim away the hair if need be. Wrap the dog in a blanket and rush him to the vet. The dog may go into shock, depending on the severity of the burn, resulting in a lowered blood pressure, which is dangerous and the reason the dog must receive immediate veterinary attention.

If a broken limb is suspected, try to keep the animal as still as possible. Wrap your pup or dog in a blanket to restrict movement and get him to the veterinarian as soon as possible. Do not move the dog's head so it is tilting backward, as this might result in blood entering the lungs.

Do not let your dog jump up and down from heights, as this can cause considerable shock to the joints. Puppies, especially, do not know when enough is enough, so you must do all their thinking for them.

Provided you apply strict hygiene to all aspects of your dog's husbandry, and you make daily checks on his physical state, you have done as much as you can to safeguard him during his most vulnerable period. Routine visits to your veterinarian are also recommended, especially while the dog is under one year of age. The vet may notice something that did not seem important to you.

Your dog will rely on you to keep him healthy and happy. Keeping your dog well cared for, taking him for regular checkups, and keeping him safe will ensure a long and happy life together.

Resources

Miniature Pinscher Club of America, Inc.
Secretary: Christine Filler
Email: MPCASecretary@minpin.org
Website: www.minpin.org/

American Kennel Club
Headquarters:
260 Madison Avenue
New York, NY 10016

Operations Center:
5580 Centerview Drive
Raleigh, NC 27606-3390

Customer Services:
Phone: (919) 233-9767
Fax: (919) 816-3627
www.akc.org

The Kennel Club
1 Clarges Street
London
W1J 8AB
Phone: 087 0606 6750
Fax: 020 7518 1058
www.the-kennel-club.org.uk

The Canadian Kennel Club
89 Skyway Avenue
Suite 100
Etobicoke, Ontario, Canada
M9W 6R4
Order Desk & Membership: 1-800-250-8040
Fax: (416) 675-6506
www.ckc.ca

The United Kennel Club, Inc.
100 E. Kilgore Road
Kalamazoo, MI 49002-5584
(616) 343-9020
www.ukcdogs.com

Index

Photo Credits

All photos by Isabelle Francais